QUESTIONS AND ANSWERS

Q A
SEALIFE
of southern Africa

Text: Susan Matthews
Illustrations: David Thorpe
Consultant: Charles Griffiths

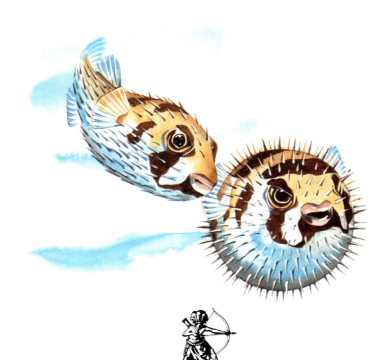

STRUIK

Contents

4. The sea
6. Raising a family
8. Growing up
10. Moving around
12. The drifters
14. Finding the way
16. Camouflage
18. Self-defence
20. Finding food
22. Filter feeders
24. Communication
26. Living together
28. Light in the sea
30. Seabirds
32. Index

Struik Publishers (Pty) Ltd
(a member of The Struik Publishing Group (Pty) Ltd)
Cornelis Struik House
80 McKenzie Street
Cape Town 8001

Reg. No.: 63/00203/07

First Published 1993

Text © Susan Matthews 1993
© Struik Publishers (Pty) Ltd 1993

All rights reserved. No part of this publication may be reproduced, stored in a retrieval system or transmitted in any form or by any means, electronic, mechanical, photocopying, recording or otherwise, without the prior written permission of the copyright owners.

Editor Sean Fraser
Designer Tracey Carstens
Illustrator David Thorpe
Typesetting by Suzanne Fortescue, Struik DTP
Reproduction by Unifoto (Pty) Ltd, Cape Town
Printed and bound by Kyodo Printing Co (Pte) Ltd, Singapore

ISBN 1 86825 352 X

Introduction

The sea covers about three quarters of the Earth's surface, and so it is home to many plants and animals. Most live in coastal waters close to land, and provide us with food such as fish, mussels, perlemoen, rock lobsters and squid. Although the open ocean is much the same all over the world, the coasts are often very different. The north-east coast of southern Africa has coral reefs with colourful fish, while further south are wide estuaries and long, sandy beaches where many sea creatures bury themselves under the sand. The rocky shores of the west coast have large colonies of seals and penguins that feed on huge shoals of fish. We can find out more about our fascinating sealife by studying the animals and plants that live on our beaches and in our rock pools.

Can you guess the names of these sea creatures? The answers are on page 32.

The sea

All living creatures in the sea are affected by the special features of seawater, such as its saltiness, temperature, tides and currents. By studying these features, we may learn more about life in the sea and on our beaches.

Why is seawater salty?

It contains large amounts of two chemicals called sodium and chloride. The salt that we add to our food is actually crystals of sodium chloride that are left behind when seawater dries up. The amount of salt in the water is called its salinity. The salinity in the seas around southern Africa hardly changes at all, but in estuaries, where fresh water from rivers mixes with seawater, the salinity varies with the tides and how fast the river is flowing. Animals and plants that live in estuaries must be specially adapted to cope with these changes.

Why is the water on our east coast warmer than on our west coast?

The Agulhas Current flows southwards down the east coast, bringing with it warm water from the hot areas around the tropics and equator. This is an extremely powerful and fast-flowing current, and animals that get caught in it are unable to escape. Along the west coast, the Benguela Current brings cold water from the south and carries it northwards. The animal communities on the west and east coasts are very different, because some animals prefer cold water while others prefer warm water.

What is upwelling?

This is the movement of seawater from deep in the ocean up to the surface. On the west coast of southern Africa, surface water is blown out to sea by south-easterly winds in spring and summer. The cold, deep water below flows up to take its place. At first this water is very clear because no phytoplankton, the sea's tiny plant life, can live in the deep ocean as it is so dark. But this water is rich in nutrients because the animals and phytoplankton living near the surface sink when they die and release nutrients as they decompose. After a few days the nutrients in the upwelled water allow phytoplankton to grow and multiply rapidly, or 'bloom', and the water becomes murky and green.

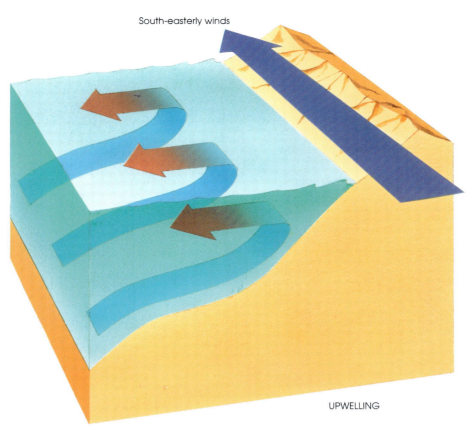

South-easterly winds

UPWELLING

Are tides affected by the moon?

Yes. Because of gravity, the moon pulls our ocean towards it, making it bulge out on the side of the Earth facing the moon. The ocean on the opposite side also bulges out as the moon and Earth spin round one another. These bulges cause high tides. As the water bulges out in these areas it is drawn away from other areas, causing low tides.

Do spring tides only occur in spring?

No. Spring tides are extra high and low tides that occur every two weeks throughout the year. They happen when the sun, moon and Earth are in line with each other. Their combined gravitational pull creates an extra large bulge of the ocean. Between the spring tides are neap tides, when high and low tides are smaller. These occur when the moon is at right angles to the sun, and their gravitational pull cancel each other out.

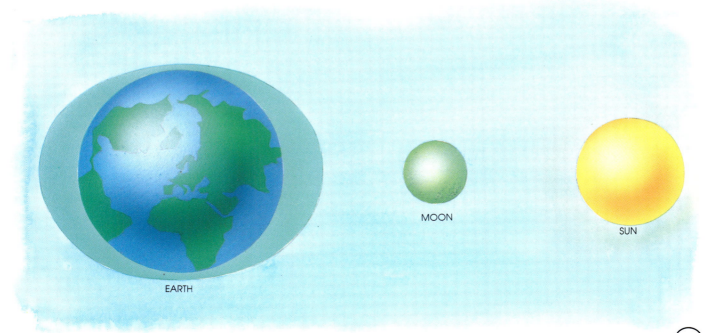

EARTH   MOON   SUN

Raising a family

All animals and plants must reproduce to ensure that their species does not become extinct. The sea can be a rather dangerous place for a small, helpless creature to live, so in many species the parents try to improve their young's chances of survival.

SEAHORSE

Why is the seahorse so special?

It is the male seahorse that gives birth to the young! The male has a pouch, rather like that of a kangaroo, which becomes swollen at the start of the breeding season. Using a long egg-laying tube, the female lays up to 200 eggs in her mate's pouch. After about six weeks the tiny seahorses are ready to hatch from the eggs in the father's pouch. The male seahorse grips a piece of seaweed with his tail and wriggles and squirms to push the babies out of the pouch. It may take him as long as two days to give birth to all the babies, after which he is absolutely exhausted.

What is a 'mermaid's purse'?

Just as a bird lays an egg, some female sharks and rays produce an eggcase called a 'mermaid's purse'. The female dogshark, for example, lays her eggs in these cases and attaches them by means of long tendrils to seaweed or soft coral. Inside the egg case there is also a large yolk, which serves as food for the growing shark. After six to nine months the young shark is large enough to break out of the case and swim weakly away.

MERMAID'S PURSE

Which little zooplankton can reproduce without mating?

The water flea. The female deposits her eggs in a brood pouch, where they all develop into identical females that are miniature versions of their mother. Some of these 'daughters' already have eggs developing inside them – even before they are big enough to be released from their mother's pouch! This means that the mother can be carrying her own granddaughters! When conditions in the sea become harsh, with cold temperatures and a shortage of food, the water flea suddenly starts producing eggs that develop into males. The males and females then mate and produce young that are better able to survive the harsh conditions.

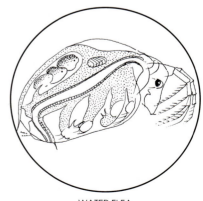

WATER FLEA

When are shrimps, crabs and crayfish 'in berry'?

When they are carrying their eggs, which look like little berries. After they have been fertilized by the male, the female lays the eggs and cements them to structures on the underside of her tail segments, called pleopods. In this way she increases their chances of surviving until they are ready to hatch. The young then float away to begin life on their own, although many still die before they reach adulthood.

CRAYFISH

CARDINALFISH

Which fish keeps its eggs in its mouth?

The cardinalfish. After the female cardinalfish lays her eggs, the male fertilizes them and then gently sucks them up into his mouth, where he incubates them until they are ready to hatch. The fish probably do this to keep the eggs safe from predators and from being swept away in the currents. Fish that have this strange behaviour are called mouthbrooders.

How do giant clams manage to mate?

Giant clams can weigh hundreds of kilograms, and are fixed in one place. Because they cannot move around to find mates, these clams reproduce by releasing their eggs and sperm, or spawn, at the same time. The spawn released by the first giant clam triggers others to release their's too. Because the spawn can get swept away by the currents, or be eaten by fish, the giant clams each produce massive amounts of spawn to make up for any that may be lost.

GIANT CLAM

Growing up

Sometimes young animals are very different from their parents, in both appearance and behaviour. This is certainly very true of many of the creatures which live in the sea and on the shore. They have an advantage in that they don't need to compete with their parents for food or a home.

HERMIT CRAB

Which crab goes house-hunting?

The hermit crab. This crab always lives in the empty shells of other animals, and as it grows it needs to move into larger and larger homes. When it sees an empty shell it feels about inside it with its nippers, to check that it is large enough and that no other animal is living there. Once the shell passes this first test the hermit crab quickly swops shells to try the new one out for fit and weight. If the shell is not suitable the crab returns to the old one before another hermit crab can steal it.

Do some periwinkles migrate as they grow?

Yes. The periwinkle *Littorina* starts life high on the shore so that it is not washed off the rocks by waves. But as the periwinkle grows it becomes strong enough to resist the waves, and so it moves down the shore and closer to the sea where there is more food to eat.

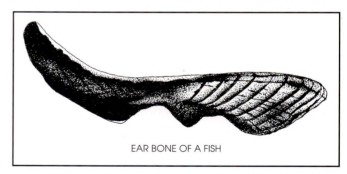
EAR BONE OF A FISH

PERIWINKLES

How can scientists tell the age of a fish?

By studying its ear bones! These little bones, called otoliths, have rings of growth, rather like those of a tree trunk. Normally, two rings are laid down each year, so by counting the number of rings, scientists can work out the age of the fish. Once they know this they can compare it to the length of the fish's body, and then work out how fast the fish grows. This is useful because it reveals when the fish will reach maturity and start producing eggs.

Do some fish have a sex change?

Yes. One example is the cleaner wrasse, which lives in small groups. Each group consists of a male and his harem of females. The male is the oldest fish in the group, and if he dies the oldest female begins to act like a male, controlling the other females in the group and also patrolling the borders of the territory. After about two weeks the fish has undergone a complete sex change, and is able to mate with females in the harem.

CLEANER WRASSE

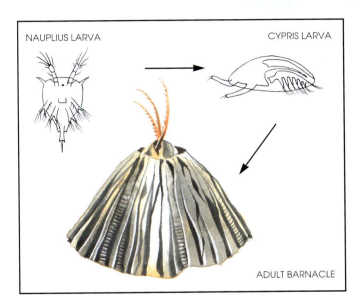
NAUPLIUS LARVA
CYPRIS LARVA
ADULT BARNACLE

Does the barnacle stand on its head?

Yes, but only when it is ready to change into an adult. A barnacle starts life as a little swimming animal, called a nauplius larva, but as it grows it moults six times before turning into a cypris larva, which is enclosed in a shell with two halves. It is now ready to change into an adult barnacle, but first it must find a place to settle. It feels around with its antennae, testing that there is enough space on the rock and that it receives enough light and water current. The larva then stands on its head and glues itself onto the rock with cement made in a gland in the antennae. It twists itself around so that the legs it once used for swimming are now kicked out into the water and used for filter-feeding. Within a few days the barnacle has become a fully formed adult, protected inside a cone-shaped shell that can be closed with a 'door' at low tide.

Why does the emperor angelfish change colour?

Like many other fishes, the emperor angelfish changes colour as it grows up. When it is young it is dark blue with white and light blue rings. This colour pattern camouflages the fish by breaking up its outline in the silvery blue water so that it confuses its predators. The adult is more colourful, with bright yellow stripes on a brown background. This is because it now has its own territory, and uses its colours to warn others not to trespass. But this bright colour pattern also makes the adult fish very obvious to predators, so it has a dark stripe hiding its vulnerable eyes.

Young
Adult
EMPEROR ANGELFISH

Moving around

Most animals must be able to move around to search for food and mates, and to escape from their enemies. We all know that fish can swim, but other creatures that live in the sea or on the seashore use some very interesting methods to move around.

FLYING FISH

Do flying fish really fly?

No, because they cannot flap their fins. But if they are being chased they leap out of the water and spread their wide fins so that they glide for up to 100 metres before they fall back into the sea. Most predators are so confused when the flying fish disappear from the sea by leaping into the air that they give up the chase.

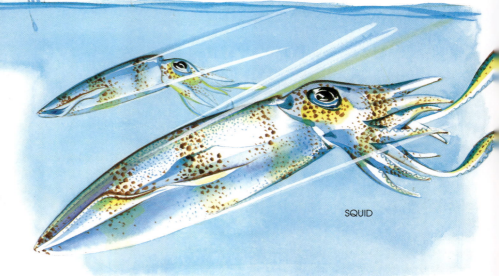

SQUID

How do squid swim so fast?

By jet propulsion! Water is drawn into the muscular mantle cavity and then forced out through a funnel. This jet of water propels the squid backwards, and because the funnel can be pointed in any direction, the squid can quickly change course if it is being chased or is trying to catch a darting fish.

SCALLOPS

Which creatures swim by clapping through the water?

Scallops. These animals are bivalves, which means that they have a shell of two halves joined by a hinge, like a mussel or a clam. They lie on their side on the sea bed and, if they are threatened, can quickly escape by clapping the two halves of the shell together. In this way, water is drawn into the shell and then quickly forced out in a jet, which propels the scallop backwards through the water.

BULLIA

Are any sea creatures surfers?

Yes, the plough shell, *Bullia*. It is a scavenger which feeds on dead and dying animals washed up on the beach, such as blue-bottles and jellyfish. At low tide it remains buried in the sand, with only its tubular siphon sticking out. As the tide rises, the plough shell emerges from the sand and uses its wide foot to help it surf ashore. Once on the beach, it can quickly detect its prey with its powerful sense of smell. After it has eaten its fill, the plough shell buries itself in the sand again and waits until the tide turns before it emerges and surfs back to its low tide position, so that it does not get stranded on the hot, dry beach.

Can mudskippers walk on land?

Yes – even though they have no legs! Mudskippers are small fish that live in tropical estuaries and mangrove swamps. They use their strong, muscular fins to skip across the mud from pool to pool. Before leaving each pool they swallow a mouthful of water which they store in their gill chambers. They can then breathe while on land by taking oxygen from this water.

MUDSKIPPERS

Why do crabs run sideways?

To stop them from tripping over their own feet! Crabs have five pairs of legs, set quite closely together, and if they tried to move forwards quickly each leg would become tangled up with the one in front of it.

Are there ghosts on our beaches?

No, but there are ghost crabs on beaches along our east coast. Ghost crabs can run at lightning speed. They only emerge from their burrows at dusk to scavenge for food cast up on the beach. Because the crabs are a rather pale colour which camouflages them against the sand, sometimes only their shadows can be seen in the moonlight as they dart in and out of their burrows and run across the sand, giving them a ghost-like appearance.

GHOST CRAB

The drifters

Some animals save their energy by drifting along on the sea's surface, rather than trying to swim against the currents. Because these animals have no way of escaping predators, most of them are coloured blue so that they are well camouflaged in the sea.

BLUE-BOTTLE

Why is a blue-bottle like an iceberg?

Because, like an iceberg, most of it is below the surface of the water, and what we see is only a small part of the whole body. The blue-bottle is actually a colony of small creatures, each with their own special function. The part that we see floating on the waves is simply called the float. It is pumped up with nitrogen and carbon monoxide gas from a small gas gland on its side. Every few minutes the float flops sideways into the water to prevent it from drying out. Below the float hang long fishing tentacles, bearing stinging cells which paralyse prey such as small fish. The tentacles can contract so that they can pass the prey to the feeding individuals of the colony. The other members of the blue-bottle colony produce young blue-bottles, which remain attached to the adult until they are large enough to break free and drift away.

What is a by-the-wind sailor?

A little animal whose proper name is *Velella*. It is a relative of the blue-bottle, but has a flat, oval float and a sail which allows it to be blown across the surface of the sea like a windsurfer. The *Velella*'s stinging tentacles allow it to catch small creatures swimming just below the surface of the water.

Who gulps air to stay afloat?

The floating sea slug, *Glaucus*. The bubble of air in its stomach keeps it afloat while it drifts across the sea surface in search of its favourite food, the blue-bottles. It can even use the stinging cells of the blue-bottles in its own tissues to defend itself from predators! The stinging cells of blue-bottles have little darts that shoot out and inject poison into prey or predators. But when *Glaucus* swallows them, the darts do not fire. Instead they pass through the wall of the gut and into the skin of the sea slug, ready to sting any attacker.

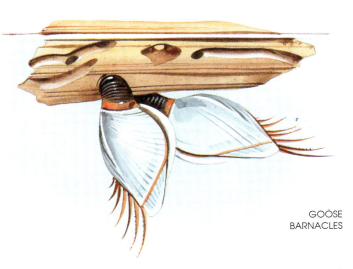

GOOSE BARNACLES

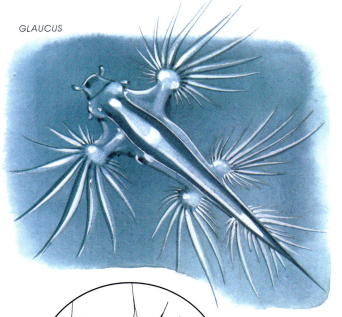

GLAUCUS

How do goose barnacles travel the world?

They get a ride on any floating object on which they can settle, using it as a raft. They are attached to the raft by means of a long, fleshy stalk, and they scoop plankton, such as diatoms, from the water using feeding structures called cirri. Some types of goose barnacle attach themselves to whales and are specially adapted so that the current created by the moving whale flows right through the barnacles, without them having to stick out their cirri. Scientists use the patterns of these barnacles to identify individual whales, allowing them to keep track of the whales' movements and to study their behaviour.

Which snail blows a raft of bubbles?

The bubble-raft shell, called *Janthina*. This pretty blue snail secretes a foam of bubbles that floats on the surface of the sea. The snail hangs upside down from this floating raft and drifts about the sea, feeding on blue-bottles and their relatives.

DIATOMS

Why do diatoms have such spiky shapes?

So that they do not sink to the bottom of the sea too quickly. Diatoms are a kind of phytoplankton, the microscopic plants in the sea, which many sea creatures rely on for food. Like all plants they need light to survive and grow, so they must stay near the surface of the sea. They cannot swim, so to prevent them from sinking to the deeper, darker reaches of the ocean, they have spiky shapes which are caught by tiny currents and keep the diatoms tumbling about near the sea's surface.

BUBBLE-RAFT SHELL

Finding the way

The sea is a huge place in which to live, with no street signs or maps to show the way. Also, sandy beaches and rocky shores must appear never-ending to the tiny creatures that live there. How do these animals find their way?

Do dolphins and whales sometimes get lost?

Yes. For some reason that is not yet understood, there are often mass strandings of dolphins or whales on shores around the world. Even if the animals are helped out to sea, many of them swim straight back to the shore again. Unfortunately many of these animals die each year.

Do young lobsters tour the ocean before settling down?

Yes. When spiny lobsters hatch they are caught up in a massive current called the south Atlantic gyre, which carries them in a huge circle between Africa and South America. Somehow they realize when they are back in their home waters again, and only then do they change into their adult form, swim out of the current and settle to the sea bed.

BEACHED PILOT WHALES

Do limpets leave trails to help them return home?

Yes. As limpets grow, their shells mould and seal perfectly around small depressions and bumps in the rocks. Each day the limpets set off to feed on algae which they scrape off the rocks. They lay down slimy trails of mucus as they go to help them glide along. Once they have eaten their fill, they return home by retracing their way along their own mucus trail, and then snuggle down into exactly the same position. The limpets may also be able to recognize tiny landmarks such as bumps and scrapes in the rock surface.

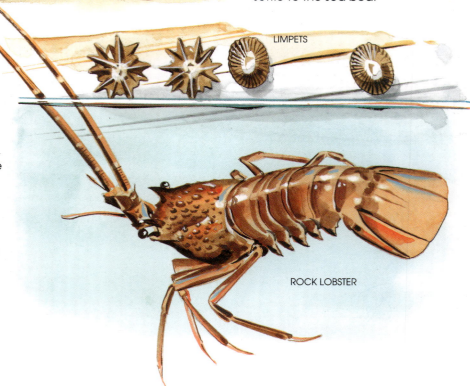

LIMPETS

ROCK LOBSTER

TURTLE HATCHLINGS

SAND HOPPERS

How do turtle hatchlings find the sea?

For many years, scientists believed that the hatchlings were attracted to the brightness of the moon shining over the sea and the sparkling waves. However, the hatchlings can also find their way on quite dark, moonless nights. It is now thought that they crawl away from the dark outlines of the sand dunes and beach vegetation, setting a course which will naturally lead them to the waves. At some turtle nesting sites in America, all the lights near the beach are switched off during the hatching season, so that the young turtles don't get confused and head in the wrong direction.

Who uses the sun as a compass?

The sand hoppers, which swarm over their favourite food of rotting kelp on the beach. They emerge from the sand at sunset, but wait until the moon rises before they hop down the beach to feed. At dawn they return to the high tide mark to bury themselves in the sand. They orientate themselves in relation to the sun's position at dusk and dawn. If the sand hoppers are moved to another beach, they lose their way and move in the wrong direction. This means that their navigating ability must be inherited from their parents and is suited only to the beach on which they were born.

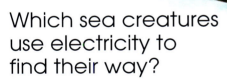
RAY

Which sea creatures use electricity to find their way?

Sharks and rays. Small structures on their heads, called the ampullae of Lorenzini, can detect weak electric fields. These allow sharks and rays to orientate themselves in relation to the Earth's electric fields. They can also detect the weak electric field generated by the activity of muscles and nerves of their prey. Recently, scientists at the Natal Sharks Board have developed a new type of shark barrier by using electricity to turn sharks away from beaches.

SHARK

Camouflage

Animals camouflage themselves to avoid attack by predators and to hide themselves while they lie in ambush for prey. They do this by either blending with their surroundings or by disguising themselves to look like other plants and animals that are ignored by predators.

What is a stonefish?

A fish that disguises itself as a stone on the sea floor. It has a rough, warty skin, and it keeps so still that it blends in perfectly with the stones around it. For this reason, someone walking in shallow water on the beach may step on it accidentally. When this happens the stonefish defends itself by injecting poison from spines along its back into the person's foot.

SPONGE CRAB

Can sand shrimps change their colour?

Yes. When these shrimps are swimming in clear water or sitting on a light background, such as sand, they are see-through except for some dark stripes which help to break up their outline. But when they sit on a dark background, such as a rock, they become a dark brown. They are able to camouflage themselves by changing colour because they have small pigment cells in the skin, which can contract to let the background colour show through or expand to darken the shrimp.

Which crab hides under a sponge?

The sponge crab. It cuts out a piece of sponge with its claws and holds it over its back with its last pair of legs, which are specially adapted for this purpose. After a while the sponge grows so that it fits around the crab. Predators mistake the crab for a sponge, which is unpleasant to eat, so they ignore the crab and look elsewhere for a meal.

SAND SHRIMP

COWRIES

How do cowries hide their shells?

By disguising them with a cloak of skin. Although cowries are famous for their beautiful shells, their shells are often covered by a fleshy layer of skin called the mantle. The blotchy colours and irregular bumps on the mantle make it look just like a piece of seaweed or allows it to blend in with the sponges on which most cowries feed. If this camouflage does not fool an alert predator, the cowrie can still protect itself by withdrawing into its shell.

Why do some fish have dark backs and pale bellies?

To make them invisible to predators. This special colour pattern is called countershading, and is common in fish which live near the sea surface. Seen from above by a predator such as a seabird, the fish blends in with the dark water below, and seen from below, the pale belly matches the silvery sunlight at the sea surface.

FLATFISH

COUNTERSHADING

Which fishes have twisted faces?

The flatfishes. When they start life, they look like normal fish and swim near the sea surface, but after a few weeks one eye has gradually moved round so that both eyes are on the same side of the head, and the front of the head has twisted. This is because the fish spends the rest of its life lying flat on its side on the sea floor, perfectly camouflaged from predators and prey. Sometimes it partly buries itself under the sand, with only its eyes sticking out, but its colours also help it to blend in with its surroundings. The upper side of the fish is a mottled brown colour, while the underside, which is hidden from view and so does not need to be camouflaged, is a plain pale colour. The flatfishes can even change colour to match the sand they are lying on. Like the sand shrimp, small pigment cells in the skin can contract to let the background colour show through, or expand to make the fish a darker colour.

Self-defence

Not all animals rely on camouflage to defend themselves from predators – some have developed dangerous weapons or strange behaviour patterns to either fight off attack or help them escape.

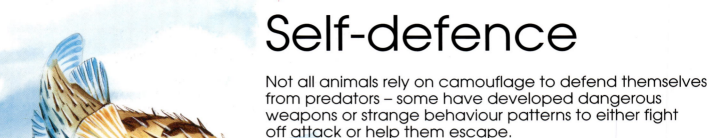
PORCUPINE FISH

Which fish is like a porcupine?

The porcupine fish, which defends itself by being prickly, just like a porcupine. When relaxed it looks much like any other fish, because the spines lie flat against the body. But if the fish is threatened it inflates itself with water, or air if it is caught and pulled out of the water, so that the spines stick out. The porcupine fish is too prickly to attack, and is now too large for most predators to swallow.

Do sea cucumbers vomit on their enemies?

No, but it sometimes looks as if they do. If they are threatened by a predator they may expel part or all of the gut. This distracts the surprised predator, and while it gobbles up the gut, the sea cucumber can escape. Luckily, the sea cucumber can grow a new gut. Some sea cucumbers cannot do this, so they entangle their attacker with a mass of sticky threads shot out from the hind end. While the attacker struggles to free itself, the sea cucumber has time to crawl away.

Do mussels sometimes tie down their attackers?

Yes. Mussels are preyed upon by whelks, which drill a hole through the mussels' shells so that they can feed on the tissues inside. They do this with their rasping 'tongue', or radula, and acid which helps soften the shell. But the mussels can sometimes defend themselves by tying down the whelks with their byssus threads, which are usually used for attaching the mussels to the rocks.

SEA CUCUMBER

How does the brittle star escape from its enemies?

By breaking off its own arm! Its five arms are much thinner than those of its relatives, the starfish, and as the name suggests, are very brittle. If a predator grabs hold of one of the arms, the brittle star breaks off the arm so that it can escape. The brittle star then immediately starts to grow a new arm in its place.

BOXER CRAB

ANEMONES

BRITTLE STAR

Which crab boxes its attackers?

The boxer crab. It carries a small anemone in each of its nippers, and if it is attacked it thrusts out one nipper after the other, like a sparring boxer. In this way it tries to sting the attacker with the anemone and make it give up the fight.

FIREFISH

Does the firefish defend itself with fire?

No, but its wavy fins look like flames, and the spines in the fins can inject a poison that causes a burning pain. Although it is related to the ugly stonefish, which camouflages itself with drab colours, the firefish uses its bright colours to warn predators that it is poisonous.

Finding food

Like all other plants, seaweeds and phytoplankton, the microscopic plants found in the sea, use sunlight to make their own food from simple chemicals in their environment. But animals cannot do this, and must eat plants or other animals to survive.

MANTIS SHRIMP

How did the mantis shrimp get its name?

It looks rather like a praying mantis insect, because it has a strong pair of special legs folded beneath its body as if it were praying, and well-developed, stalked eyes. Most mantis shrimps wait at the entrance of their burrows for passing prey, such as shrimp and fish, which they spear with spines on the special legs. Others stalk their prey and use the powerful legs to smash the shells of clams and crabs, which they then carry back to the burrow to eat.

Which snails shoot their prey with a poison arrow?

The cone shells. The teeth of these pretty sea snails have become modified into hundreds of tiny arrows which they store in a sac inside their body. When they find prey, such as a worm or a fish, they shoot stab or one of these arrows into the prey. Poison carried within the hollow arrow paralyses the prey and, because the snail is then in no danger of being injured in a fight, it can swallow prey almost as big as itself!

CONE SHELL

PARROTFISH

Which fish crunches coral?

The parrotfish. It gets its name because it is so colourful and has strong teeth which are all fused together to look like a parrot's beak. It uses these teeth to bite off chunks of coral and chew them up so that it can feed on the soft coral polyps and on small algae that live in the tissues of the coral.

Do perlemoen trap their food?

Yes. Young perlemoen feed by scraping tiny plants, or algae, off the rocks with a toothed 'tongue' called a radula. But as they get older they trap drifting pieces of kelp by raising the front of the shell and then clamping down tightly over the kelp. During stormy weather, when strong currents sweep through the kelp bed, the perlemoen may also clamp down on the tip of a swaying frond of kelp. Sometimes a number of perlemoen work together to trap a large frond of kelp, which is then shared by them all.

SPINY STARFISH

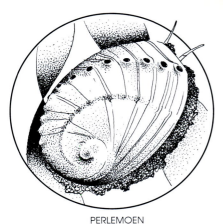
PERLEMOEN

Can a starfish eat through its stomach?

Yes. The favourite food of the spiny starfish are mussels, which protect themselves from most predators by clamping together the two halves of their shell. But this large starfish has hundreds of tube feet on the underside of each of its five arms, which can exert a powerful grip. They can prise open a mussel shell until there is enough space for the starfish to push its stomach into the gap and release digestive juices that break down the mussel's flesh. The food can then be sucked up into the starfish's gut.

Why is a goatfish like a billy goat?

It has two long fleshy whiskers, called barbels, hanging down from the chin. The goatfish wiggles the barbels, which are equipped with special taste organs, in the sand to search for prey such as worms, shrimps and small fish. If the barbels disturb prey the goatfish snatches them up into its mouth. Other fish often follow closely behind to eat any prey that the goatfish misses.

Do dolphins zap their prey with sonar?

Yes. Sonar is a method of location using echoes. By bouncing sounds off a target and analysing how quickly they echo back, dolphins can locate schools of fish. They can fine-tune this echolocation by producing about 500 click sounds every second as they get closer to their unsuspecting prey. It is also thought that dolphins can stun fish with these high-pitched clicks so that they are easier to catch. During a feeding frenzy a dolphin can switch the sonar off instantly if another dolphin swims in front of it, so that it does not hurt its companions.

GOATFISH

Filter feeders

Many animals in the sea do not move about to search for food, but wait for tiny particles of food to float to them. They then use special filters to sift the food from the water. These filter-feeders either eat the ocean's microscopic plant life (phytoplankton), tiny animals (zooplankton), or pieces of dead and rotting plant and animal material, called detritus.

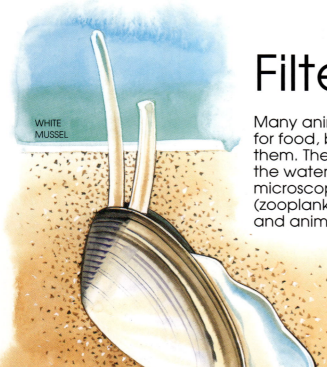

WHITE MUSSEL

Which mussel feeds through a straw?

The white mussel. It digs into the sand until it is hidden below the surface, and extends two siphons into the water. The shorter of the two, called the inhalent siphon, is like a straw because it sucks in water. Phytoplankton and detritus in the water are trapped by the mussel's gills, and the water is then forced out through the longer, exhalent siphon. The inhalent siphon has a sieve across its opening to prevent sand from clogging up the gills.

How do paddles help the mud prawn feed?

They help it filter food from the water. The mud prawn wedges itself into its U-shaped burrow and uses the paddle-like pleopods under its tail to force a current of water through the burrow. Plankton and detritus are filtered out of this water by fringed hairs on the prawn's mouthparts and its first pair of legs.

MUD PRAWN

Did you know?

Sometimes mussels are killed when they filter-feed large amounts of poisonous phytoplankton during a red tide. Red tides are caused when some phytoplankton, called dinoflagellates, multiply rapidly or 'bloom' during certain ideal conditions. Poisonous dinoflagellates can paralyse white mussels, which are then washed up on beaches. If these mussels are eaten, they can paralyse or even kill a person. But most red tides are caused by dinoflagellates which are not poisonous, although they can still kill mussels by clogging their gills.

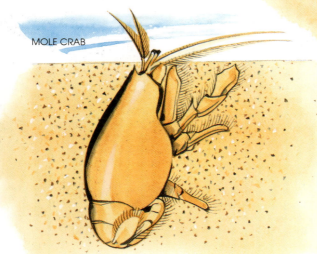

MOLE CRAB

Which crab filter-feeds with its antennae?

The mole crab. This strange-looking crab lives in the surf zone on beaches in Natal, and migrates up and down the beach with the waves as the tide rises and falls. It uses its spade-like legs to dig backwards into the sand, until only its stalked eyes and two pairs of antennae are visible. These antennae, which are fringed with hairs, are held out to filter food particles from the water.

What is a feather duster worm?

FEATHER DUSTER WORMS

SEA SQUIRTS

A filter-feeding worm which looks like a feather duster. It is also called a fan worm, because its feathery filaments are in the shape of a fan and are all you can usually see of the worm. The rest of the body is protected inside a tube which the worm builds from sand grains mixed with mucus. Particles in the water are trapped on the filaments, which are covered with tiny hairs that sweep the particles into a groove leading to the mouth. This groove sorts the food – small particles are carried straight to the mouth, while medium-sized particles are stored in a pair of sacs near the mouth until they can be used to fix the tube. Large particles cannot fit into the groove, so are rejected.

Why do sea squirts sometimes squirt?

To spit out water after they have filtered out their food. These creatures are sometimes seen squirting water quite high into the air at low tide. The most familiar sea squirt is the large red-bait, *Pyura*, which is often used by fishermen as bait, but some sea squirts are small and transparent, and live in colonies. Sea squirts feed by sucking up water through an inhalent siphon into the pharynx, a sieve-like structure dotted with holes. As the water flows out through the holes, food particles are trapped in a sticky mucus and are then swept into the sea squirts' stomach. The filtered water is then squirted out through an exhalent siphon.

Which are the largest filter feeders?

Baleen whales. These whales do not have teeth, but comb-like structures called baleen plates which hang from their upper jaw. Most of these whales feed on krill, a shrimp-like zooplankton which in turn feeds on phytoplankton. After taking a mouthful of seawater, the whale uses its tongue to force the water out through the baleen plates so that the krill are trapped against them. The blue whale, which is the largest animal in the world, eats about four tons of krill every day!

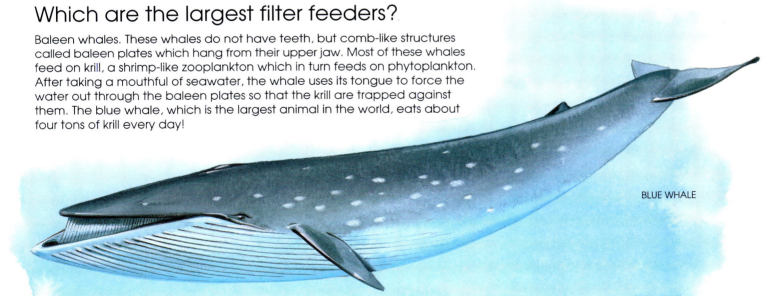

BLUE WHALE

Communication

Animals need to pass information on to each other for many different reasons. They may want to scare other animals off their territories, attract and impress a mate, or warn others about approaching danger, but they all have a unique way of communicating with each other.

SEALS

How does a mother seal find her pup?

She calls the pup to her. About a week after giving birth the mother seal has to leave her pup for a while so that she can return to the sea to feed. While she is away her pup moves around playing with other 'orphans'. When she returns, she has to find her pup amongst thousands of identical-looking pups, so she moves through the colony, calling loudly as she goes. Several pups may run towards her, all hoping that it is their mother that has returned, but she sniffs each one until she recognizes the smell of her own pup.

Can dolphins and whales 'talk'?

Yes, they have their own 'languages'. Whales communicate with squeaks and moans that can travel long distances through the water to call males and females together during the breeding season. Dolphins communicate with high-pitched clicks and whistles. Although these sounds don't travel as far as the whales' songs, they are an important form of communication for dolphins. When they are swimming in a school, they use clicks to send messages to each other, but as they get more excited during feeding frenzies or encounters with other dolphin schools they whistle constantly.

BOTTLE-NOSED DOLPHINS

How do pistol shrimps warn off intruders?

These shrimps have one nipper that is much larger than the other, and which they can snap closed to make a popping sound, rather like when we snap our fingers. Pistol shrimps control a territory around their burrows, and if another pistol shrimp crosses the borders of the territory, the loud snap from the nipper warns the unwelcome intruder that it is trespassing.

Do fiddler crabs wave at their mates?

Yes. Although female fiddler crabs have two equal-sized claws, males have one claw which is much bigger than the other and which becomes brightly coloured during the breeding season. The male waves this claw up and down to attract the attention of a female, and to lure her into his burrow so that they can mate. Several different species of fiddler crabs may live on the same beach, but they must only mate with crabs of their own species. Each species therefore has its own distinctive way of waving, so that females can recognize males of their species.

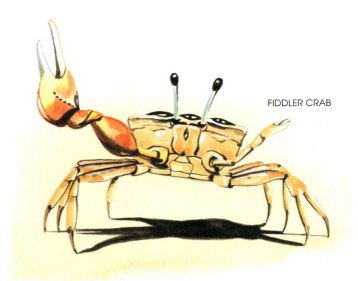
FIDDLER CRAB

Can an octopus flush with excitement?

Yes. If it sees prey, such as a crab, it gets so excited that it flushes a darker colour. A male octopus may also use this colour-changing ability to impress a female during courtship. However, if the octopus is scared by an animal larger than itself, it pales in fear. It flattens its body and turns almost white except for dark patches round its eyes. This makes the octopus seem larger than it actually is, which might frighten away the attacker. The octopus is able to communicate with colour in this way because it has small pigment cells in its skin, which are stretched or contracted by tiny muscles.

COWFISH

CRAB
OCTOPUS

Why do cowfish dance together?

It is part of their courtship display. When the male cowfish is ready to mate he swims into the female's territory and rocks back and forth in front of her. The female then leads him in a slow, spiral dance up towards the surface of the sea to show that she is interested in him too. When they are just below the surface, they turn tail to tail and the female releases her eggs while the male releases his sperm. They then swim off in different directions. These fish are named after cows because they have little horns on the front of their heads.

MORAY EEL
SPINY LOBSTER

Living together

Many organisms in the sea live together in close relationships that often last their entire lives. In some of these relationships, both partners benefit by helping each other. This is called mutualism. In others, one partner benefits while the other is not affected in any way, and this is called commensalism.

Do spiny lobsters have a bodyguard?

Yes. On the east coast spiny lobsters, which are the favourite food of octopuses, often share their shelters with a moray eel. If an octopus tries to pull a lobster from its shelter, the moray eel attacks the octopus and eats it! Both animals benefit from this relationship because, while the lobster has its own bodyguard, the moray eel just has to wait for its meal to come along. Some lobsters don't have their own bodyguards, but if they are attacked they make a shrill noise by rubbing the bases of their antennae against a ridge on their hard shell. When the moray eel hears this alarm call, it goes rushing to the rescue.

Does the blind shrimp have a housemate?

Yes. Some types of gobies, which are small fish, share a burrow in the sandy sea bed with the blind shrimp. The goby stands guard at the entrance to the burrow while the shrimp cleans and repairs their home. The shrimp only comes out to dump a pile of rubble when a flick from the goby's tail tells it that it is safe to do so. While it is outside the burrow, the shrimp keeps in contact with the goby with its long antennae. If danger threatens, the goby dives down the burrow, closely followed by its friend. In return for being a lookout for the shrimp, the goby has a safe place to live.

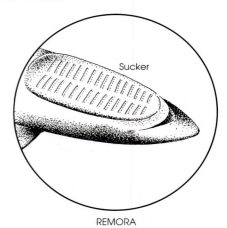
Sucker
REMORA

GOBY
BLIND SHRIMP

Do some fish really hitch-hike?

Yes. The remora is a strange fish which has a large sucker on the top of its head with which it attaches itself to a shark. Not only does the remora get a free ride with the shark, and so does not waste its own energy by swimming, it also steals pieces of the shark's food! The shark does not seem to mind the remora, but it doesn't get anything in return for its generosity.

What is a clown fish?

A colourful fish that lives on large tropical sea anemones. Although other fish get stung by the stinging cells on the anemones' tentacles, the clown fish is quite safe. It is thought that something in the slimy mucus layer covering the fish prevents the stinging cells from firing their poison darts. The clown fish is protected from predators that are scared of getting stung by the anemone, and it pays for its keep by clearing bits of shell and sand from between the anemone's tentacles.

Which shrimp sets up a service station?

The cleaner shrimp. It attracts the attention of fish by waving its antennae at them, and then cleans wounds and picks parasites and dead tissue off the fishes' skin or even inside their mouth with its pincers. The fish are so grateful that they always avoid eating the cleaner shrimp, which they recognize by its bright colours. Sometimes when the cleaner shrimp is very busy, a number of fish can be seen waiting their turn for service.

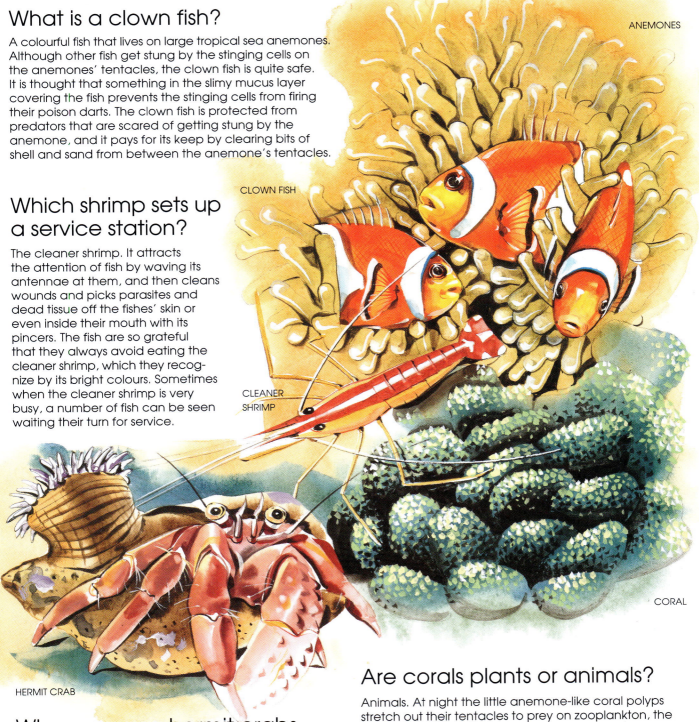

Why are some hermit crabs kidnappers?

They prise anemones off the rocks and transfer them to their own shells. In this way the hermit crabs are protected from predators by the stinging cells on the tentacles of the anemones. The anemones do not mind being kidnapped, because they are carried around to new areas which might have more food, and also share scraps of food caught by the hermit crab.

Are corals plants or animals?

Animals. At night the little anemone-like coral polyps stretch out their tentacles to prey on zooplankton, the tiny animal life floating in the sea. But during the day the polyps stay inside their 'skeleton', and rely on microscopic plant cells living within their tissues to provide them with food. Like all plants, these cells need light for photosynthesis, the process by which they make food. This is the reason why coral reefs are only found in clear, shallow waters, where there is enough light for the plant cells. In return for sharing their food with the coral, the plant cells have a place to live and use the waste products of the coral for photosynthesis.

Light in the sea

Like fireflies and glow-worms on land, some animals in the sea are luminescent, which means that they are able to produce light. They may use this special ability to defend themselves against predators, to find food, or even to attract a mate.

How do some deep-sea squid escape predators?

They confuse them by squirting out a cloud of glowing ink. Other squid use black ink to surprise their enemies, but this would be useless to an animal that lives in the darkest depths of the ocean. Instead, these deep-sea squid rely on the luminescent cloud, which probably dazzles the predator as well as distracts it while the squid escapes.

Which fish uses light as bait?

The deep-sea anglerfish, which lives in the depths of the ocean. Because it is so dark down there, some fish are unable to hunt by sight. The anglerfish solves this problem in a very strange way. It has a luminous organ dangling from a 'fishing rod' held in front of its mouth, and when a curious animal such as a shrimp or small fish comes to investigate the light, it is snatched up by the powerful jaws of the anglerfish.

DEEP-SEA SQUID

Why do waves sometimes sparkle at night?

Floating in the waves are large numbers of a dinoflagellate called *Noctiluca*, which means 'night light'. These are tiny, single-celled organisms which are only about one millimetre across. They are always present in the sea, but certain ideal conditions make them multiply very quickly, or bloom, so that millions bob about in the waves. As the waves break, tiny granules inside *Noctiluca* are stimulated to flash with light, so that the waves seem to sparkle at night.

DEEP-SEA ANGLERFISH

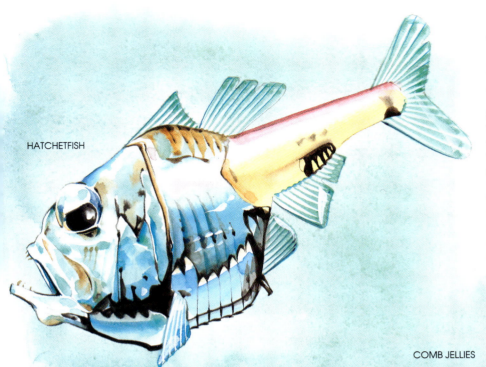

Why do hatchetfish have portholes of light?

So that their predators cannot see them from below. These fish live fairly deep in the ocean, where the light filtering down from the sea surface is dim. Light from the 'portholes' on the underside of the fish matches this dim light, ensuring that when seen from below the dark shape of the fish is not silhouetted against the light background of the sea surface above.

Do comb jellies have fairy lights?

No, but it sometimes looks as if they do because they flicker with different colours. Comb jellies get their name from the rows of small hair-like structures called cilia, which 'comb' the water and propel the animal forwards. In the walls of the gut there are tiny granules that are luminescent, and because comb jellies are transparent, they light up the comb rows as they beat.

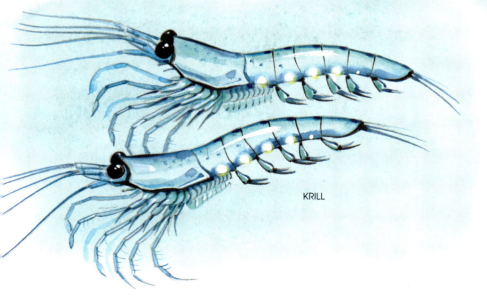

Why do krill flash when frightened?

To escape from their enemies. They have small light-producing organs, called photophores, on various parts of their body. If the krill is being chased, the bright flash stops the predator in its tracks, giving the krill time to escape. It also flashes each time it changes direction, so although the confused predator may snatch at the light, it cannot catch the darting krill.

Seabirds

Although seabirds all breed on land, they depend on the sea for their food and so are very important in the marine food chain. They have many different ways of catching their prey. They may dive or swim after fish, or even pick shellfish or other small animals off the rocks. All seabirds are adapted in unique ways for their particular lifestyle.

FLAMINGOS

Which bird walks in circles for its food?

The flamingo. It feeds in shallow lakes and estuaries by shuffling its feet around in a circle to stir up the mud. As the small organisms living in the mud swarm to the surface, the flamingo holds its bill upside down in the water and moves its thick tongue to and fro. This action sucks water through the bill, which is lined with a fringe of hairs. The organisms are trapped against this fringe, from where they are licked off and swallowed.

Are kelp gulls really thieves?

Yes. They steal each other's food because it is easier than searching for their own. They often run after each other on the ground, trying to tear food from each other's beaks. Some are even more sneaky. Kelp gulls feed on mussels, which they crack open by dropping them from the air onto the rocks below. Often another gull will swoop down and steal the mussel before its owner can land.

Why does the pelican have a throat pouch?

To scoop up fish. When the pelican chases a fish it opens its beak underwater and the pouch balloons out to surround the prey. The pelican lifts its head out of the water and tilts its beak down to drain out all the water, before throwing back its head and swallowing the fish.

KELP GULLS

PELICAN

Which bird dive-bombs fish?

The gannet. It dives for fish from as high as 30 metres in the air, and hits the sea with great force. The gannet has a number of adaptations for this diving habit. The bones in the skull are strengthened to absorb some of the impact when the bird hits the water, and the neck and throat area are cushioned by air sacs below the skin which are filled with air before the dive. The horny coverings over the nasal openings prevent water from being forced into them, while the eyes are protected by membranes which flick over them as soon as the bird hits the water.

Do oystercatchers only eat oysters?

No. In fact their favourite foods are mussels and limpets. By jabbing between the two halves of a mussel shell with their sharp beak, the oystercatchers can cut through the muscle which holds the two halves together. They then use their beaks like scissors to open the mussels so that they can eat the flesh inside. Oystercatchers prise limpets off the rocks by using the beak as a lever, but if the limpet won't budge they hit the edge of the shell with their closed beak to dislodge the limpet.

Do cormorants drip-dry?

Yes. The feathers of cormorants are less waterproof than those of other seabirds. This means that cormorants cannot stay in the water for very long, as their feathers become waterlogged, allowing the bird to get cold. After swimming and diving after prey, such as crabs and fish, they dry themselves off by standing on the rocks with their wings stretched out.

Do penguins fly underwater?

Yes. Although their wings are too short for flying through the air, penguins chase fish underwater by flapping their wings to propel themselves rapidly forward. Their bodies are streamlined, which helps to make them fast swimmers, and they have webbed feet which are used for steering.

Index

A
Agulhas Current 4
anemone **19**, **27**
anglerfish **28**

B
baleen plates 23
baleen whale 23
barbels 21
barnacle **9**, 13
  cypris larva **9**
  nauplius larva **9**
Benguela Current 4
blind shrimp **26**
'bloom' 22, 28
blue-bottle 11, **12**, 13
blue whale 23
bottle-nosed dolphin **24**
boxer crab **19**
brittle star **19**
bubble-raft shell 13
Bullia 11
by-the-wind-sailor **12**

C
camouflage 9, 12, 16, 17
cardinalfish **7**
clam **7**, 10
  giant **7**
cleaner shrimp **27**
cleaner wrasse **9**
clown fish **27**
coloration 9, 17, 25, 27, 29
comb jelly **29**
commensalism 26
communication 24, 25
cone shell **20**
coral 20, **27**
cormorant **31**
countershading 17
cowfish **25**
cowrie **17**
crab 7, **8**, **11**, **16**, **19**, **22**, **25**, 27
crayfish **7**
currents 4, 5, 21

D
diatom 13
dinoflagellates 22, 28
dogshark 6
dolphin 14, 21, **24**

E
eel **26**
emperor angelfish **9**
estuary 4, 30

F
fan worm **23**
feather duster worm **23**
feathers 31
fiddler crab **25**
filter-feeding 9, 22, 23
firefish **19**
flamingo 30
flatfish **17**
flying fish **10**

G
gannet **31**
ghost crab **11**
giant clam **7**
Glaucus **13**
goatfish **21**
goby **26**
goose barnacle **13**
gull **30**

H
hatchetfish **29**
hermit crab **8**, **27**

J
Janthina **13**
jellyfish **11**

K
kelp 21
kelp gull **30**
krill 23, **29**

L
light 28, 29
limpet **14**, 31
Littorina **8**
luminescence 28, 29

M
mantis shrimp **20**
mermaid's purse **6**
mole crab **22**
moon 5, 15
moray eel **26**
mouthbrooders **7**
mud prawn **22**
mussel 10, 18, 21, **22**, 30, 31
mutualism 26

N
Natal 22
  Sharks Board 15
nippers 8, 19, 24
Noctiluca 28
nutrients 5

O
octopus **25**, 26
otolith **8**
oyster 31
oystercatcher **31**

P
parrotfish **20**
pelican **30**
penguin **31**
periwinkle **8**
perlemoen **21**
photophores 29
photosynthesis **27**
phytoplankton 5, 13, 20, 22, 23
pistol shrimp **24**
plankton 13
pleopods **7**, 22
plough shell **11**
poison 13, 16, 20, 22, 27

porcupine fish **18**
praying mantis 20
Pyura 23

R
radula 18, 21
ray 6, **15**
red-bait 23
remora **26**

S
sand hopper **15**
sand shrimp **16**
scallop **10**
sea cucumber **18**
sea slug **13**
sea squirt **23**
seabirds 30, 31
seahorse **6**
seal **24**
seawater 4, 5, 23
seaweed 6, 17, 20
shark 6, **15**, 26
shells 8, 17, 18, 20
shrimp 7, **16**, **20**, **24**, 26, 27
siphon 11, 22, 23
sonar 21
spiny lobster **14**, **26**
spiny starfish **21**
sponge **16**, 17
sponge crab **16**
squid **10**, **28**
starfish 19, **21**
stonefish **16**, 19
strandings **14**

T
tides 5
turtle **15**

U
upwelling **5**

V
Velella **12**

W
water flea **6**
waves 8, 15
whale 13, **14**, 23, 24
  baleen 23
  blue 23
  pilot **14**
whelk 18
white mussel **22**

Z
zooplankton 6, 22, 23

Answers
1. Crab
2. Brown mussels
3. Octopus
4. Perlemoen
5. Red roman
6. Rock lobster